MW01641284

The Perfect Triangle

The Perfect Triangle

Three Sides to A Story

Bernard Snyder

Library of Congress Control Number:		2019906835
ISBN:	Hardcover	978-1-7960-3546-9
	Softcover	978-1-7960-3545-2
	eBook	978-1-7960-3544-5

Print information available on the last page.

Rev. date: 06/06/2019

To order additional copies of this book, contact:
Xlibris
1-888-795-4274
www.Xlibris.com
Orders@Xlibris.com
796975

Dedication

This book was written and dedicated to two of the strongest people I know, my cousin Ervin Miller Sr. and his lovely wife Bridgette. These two are the most genuine, loving, and caring people I've ever met in my lifetime. Nick and I lived together for quite some time in Savannah Georgia, along with my other cousin, Raymond Cannon. We went out together, partied together, stayed up all night talking about life in general, he even chose me to be his best man in his wedding, and to this very day, we still have a great bond. Unfortunately, almost two years ago Nick was involved in a car accident that almost took his life. God spared him another chance to grace us with his presence and show the rest of us what happens when you keep a positive attitude, a sense of determination and the importance of having someone at your side that loves you. God knew as strong as Nick was, he would need someone loyal, mentally tough, and equally as strong during this time. Nick has a great support system, a loving family, a very supportive group of sisters that would go a step and beyond for him., along with his two sons that stood by his side throughout. But I believe God's most precious gift to Nick was Bridgette, his loving wife for as many years as I can count. For Bridgette, it hasn't been easy. I know this. What she has shown through this entire ordeal cannot be expressed in words alone. I commend her. Not just for her constant care and love for Nick, but her positive faith and upbeat spirit through all of this. I chose to dedicate this book to both Nick and Bridgette. For simply being two of the strongest, most loving and deserving people I know!

By Bernard Snyder

'Special Note

Unlike my first four books, I've decided to add a few pictures to this novel. These pictures don't necessarily coincide, correlate, or have any significance to the story whatsoever, but they all have a story of their own. On another note, I could not let this opportunity pass without giving thanks to an amazing group of people for making this Autobiography what it is. Valeria Tannuzzi, you are an amazing talent. I appreciate how you brought imagination and beauty together to create the book's cover. Words can't fully describe how amazing you truly are. Thank you so very much for everything you've done. Laurie McCall, you are one of the most incredible people I know. Aside from being an amazing author, photographer, wife and mother, you inspired me to write this Autobiography. You were the first to hear my complete story. It was your encouraging words that brought this book to life. When I read your book "*Sway of the Siren*" I instantly thought, and still think it is one of the best books ever written. And to have had the opportunity to speak with you on a regular basis, I realize you are as impressive as your printed words. LaDonna Woods. Though we've never actually met in person, you've been an inspiration to me for better than two years. You broadened my imagination and allowed me to write 'outside the box'. Though we live many miles apart, I cherish the fact that you and I have become closer than neighbors. Many thanks. Anthony Grant, I consider you are an awesome friend. Aside from being one of the best pool players I've ever met, you are also one of the most genuine people I know. I appreciate you more than words can say. So I'll just say "Thanks a Million" my friend. I would like to thank the entire staff at Bluffton's Library for assisting me in so many ways. I would like to thank the entire staff at Hilton Head Island's Library for your attentiveness, professionalism, and kindness throughout my process as a writer. And last but definitely not least, I would like to give thanks to Vanessa G. Your talent is far greater than you know. Sometimes we put the gift God gave us on the back burner for things we think are more important, not realizing anything God-given is a blessing in itself. There's a whole world of young people out there that wish they had the talent God granted you. Please use your amazing gift to inspire that little girl or boy that continues to watch in amazement as you blossom into the artist God created you to be. Thanks again to each and every one of you.

"Special Thanks"

'As always, I would like to give thanks to God first and foremost. People often tell me that my thank you page in my previous books all have the same pattern. Some say they seem too redundant. I've been told I should change things up a bit. Well, here's why I won't change a single thing. At a very young age I lost both parents. I wondered daily how I would make it in this cruel place called life. I was only five years old but I dreamed a lot. All of my dreams were big. Some of them I thought were too farfetched, others I thought were impossible. And now that I am older, I reflect back on those same dreams and smile. I smile because every one of those dreams came true. I can't speak for anyone else, but I know who made all of those things possible. I am also fully aware of who it was that carried me when my parents weren't able to. I know who it was that showed me a different avenue when I was two steps away from crossing the wrong path. I understand who provided me strength when I was almost at the point of giving up. Those times when people did me wrong, I kept my head up because I was certain I'd be given the strength and intestinal fortitude to keep going. So when people say to me I should change, or asks me why do I always put God first, my answer is quite simple, how can I not.'

Chapter One

Nathan

It was March 1998, Saint Patrick's Day weekend. I was having a drink with my friend, Jay, at 'The G-Spot Lounge', when two women walked in, looked around, then sat at a table directly behind me. One of them was short, the other much taller, 5' 10 to be exact, and by far the most beautiful woman I'd ever laid eyes on in my lifetime. I could tell by the way they looked around, they were either tourists or unfamiliar to the area. I jokingly whispered to Jay that, if I was five inches taller, I would purchase a diamond ring and make the taller one my wife. Jay and I laughed for a brief moment. Suddenly, I felt a tap on my shoulder. It was the shorter of the two women that had just sat at the table behind me. The young lady introduced herself as 'Patrice', and said that her friend Florence went to dance, but sent her over to invite me to join them at their table by the time the song ends. Totally surprised, I told Patrice to make certain she didn't accidentally choose the wrong person, because even in my wildest dream, I couldn't grow five to ten inches in height before the song ends. Patrice smiled and said, "My friend doesn't make mistakes and neither do I, so should we be expecting you shortly?" I said, "Sure, give me a few minutes, I will join you." As Patrice slowly walked back to her table, I thought I would ask Jay what he thought these ladies wanted. Jay assumed it was the tailored suit I was wearing. He said, "Those

women probably think you're either a Longshoreman with a lot of money, or some type of drug lord and would like you to pay their tab at the end of the night." I pondered over Jay's idea for all of five seconds, but decided I would go over and join the ladies just to nip my curiosity. I told Jay I would return later to fill him in on what transpires. I joined Patrice at their table and took a seat. As Patrice was placing an order of drinks with a server, her friend was approaching from the dance floor with the biggest grin on her face. The way she was grinning, I thought she must've realized how short I actually was. Nonetheless, we introduced ourselves to each other and instantly started a conversation. The gentleman Florence had danced with was in arm's reach as she and I talked and talked. Patrice sat quietly sipping on her drink. I couldn't help but notice Florence had somewhat of an accent and she was even more beautiful than I initially thought. For a split second, I was somewhat mesmerized by her beauty. I felt she was an angel sent from heaven.

Florence and I talked all night long. Jay must've seen how preoccupied I was, because he came over to tell me he was leaving and he and I would catch up at another time. I introduced Jay to the ladies, he shook their hands, and because he had to work early the next morning, his night at the bar had to end. So Florence and I talked about everything it seems. She told me that she and Patrice had rented a suite across town and tonight was their final night in Savannah. She mentioned also that she was in a crazy long-term relationship at one point in her life, and that she wouldn't wished what she'd been through on anyone. Somewhere along our conversation, Florence mentioned she didn't have any pets, but her admiration for frogs go way beyond words. I couldn't help but ask her, "Why frogs dear?" "To be honest, I was never able to answer that, but I even have one tattooed on my thigh." Florence said. Weird I thought, but our conversation was so enlightening, I didn't want to ruin it by judging her based solely on her likes or dislikes. I noticed also that, the tall gentleman that danced with Florence earlier was still in arm's length of her this entire time as she and I talked the night away. I was uncertain about his position. So I thought I would excuse myself for a moment to see if I could determine what trick he may have had up his sleeves. As I got up to leave, Florence said to me, "Where do you think you're going? I invited you over here, so everyone else is nonexistent." I instantly thought this woman is either a former colonel in the military or someone that knows what she wants and isn't shy about it. Needless to say, Florence and I sat and talked throughout the evening. As the night started to come to an end, Florence asked me if I would walk with her to her car. I gladly agreed. As we walked along the dimly lit sidewalk, with Patrice a few feet behind, I noticed a crowd of folks staring at this Gold, custom-made Volvo." It's the most unique Volvo I'd ever seen," one guy yelled out. One of the admirers looking at it said, "I bet it has a remote control that actually controls everything on the dashboard." The gentlemen's comment caught my attention as well. I asked Florence if we could pause for a moment to check this car out. Florence smiled and

nodded her head in agreement. As I looked over the amazing finish and well-maintained interior of the car, Florence just patiently waited to the side. I mentioned to Florence I'd seen enough and we should go. Florence smiled and said, "We actually don't really have to go anywhere dear, this car happens to be mine." Well, I wanted to tell her that her car was almost as beautiful as she was, but I thought I'd save that compliment for another day. As she approached the driver's side door, I opened her door and slid her one of my business cards, with my picture and phone number attached. "Hopefully, this will help us keep in touch." I said. Florence smiled, took the card and said "I will call to check to see if you haven't given me a bogus number." I said, "I look forward to your test.

My two-bedroom apartment was only two blocks away. I wanted to ask them if they'd like to spend the night at my place, but I realize they would have to drive across town to get their belongings and then drive all the way back, so instead, I thought it would be wiser to call the number to their suite, which Florence had given me earlier at the bar, to check on them and make sure they were okay. I was more than happy to know that they had. Florence was elated that I'd call her suite. She told me how interesting our conversation was, and that if I'd like to drive over to see her before she left in the morning, it wouldn't be a problem. I was flattered but decided I would take a rain-check instead.

Chapter Two

Three Weeks Later

Nathan

I was having a quiet weekend when, I got a call from Florence. She mentioned that she was bored and she would like to visit me in Savannah. I was pleasantly surprised and told her it would be my pleasure to have her come over. I know her hometown of Beacon was more than two and a half hours away, so I cleaned my apartment thoroughly and prepared a hearty meal. I'd mentioned to Florence three weeks earlier that I was a chef, so I thought I would put something nice together that would be pleasing to her eyes as well as her appetite. I prepared Beef Wellington, Oven-roasted potatoes with a hint of garlic, fresh Green Beans sautéed in Shallots, and for dessert I prepared Banana Frosty. About three hours later, Florence pulled onto my drive-way. She looked rather different than when we first met three weeks ago. Her skin seemed darker, her hair was straight as an arrow and more noticeable than anything, she was soaking and wet. I hesitantly asked her was everything okay. Florence said "Yes all is well, except for the fact that my AC compressor went out on me during my drive over, and for more than two hours, I had to drive with the windows down." Florence said she'd contacted a dealership and got quoted a price of fifteen hundred dollars to have a compressor replaced. She mentioned also

that she'd spoken to her dad, and he will have it taken care of as soon as she gets back to Beacon S.C.. I took her belongings from the back seat of her car, invited her in, and told her whatever she'd like in the 'fridge', feel free to it. Florence grabbed a bottled-water and began to share with me how beautiful of a drive it was despite the scorching temperatures. She said, "I would've gotten here sooner, but I decided to take a break at the beautiful Angus farm in Jetson S.C. to soak in the tranquil setting." Florence had an amazing sense of humor. She told me when she got out of her car at the farm, two of the cows were at a nearby fence eating grass, when one of the cows said to the other one, "Let's move elsewhere, this bitch looks hungry." I found her humor quite entertaining to say the least.

Florence said she could smell my dinner as soon as she drove up the drive-way. I said "freshen up and as soon as you get done, we could 'pig out." Florence showered, we blessed the food, then began feasting. Florence took a bite of the Wellington, paused for a split second, looked under the table, and then asked, "Where is she?" I asked "Who are you referring to?" Florence said, "I am looking for the maid that cooked all of this." I smiled and told Florence I would be the only maid she would find in this house today.

Florence was very inquisitive. She asked for a detailed description of how I made each dish. I didn't have a problem sharing my recipes with her. Florence thought it was amazing that I'd learned everything I knew about cooking by watching other Chefs I've worked with over the years. She said to me, "No one cooks this good just by watching." I said "Florence, I could make up another story just to please you, but it wouldn't be the truth." Florence then said "The way to my heart is through a hearty meal and if you can actually cook, you might very well be my heart string." I simply smiled and prepared her dessert. While we were eating, I decided to ask Florence about her AC compressor again to get a better understanding. Florence said "I'm not worried about it anymore. I've already spoken to my dad. He's going to have it taken care of as soon as I get back home." After we were done eating, Florence wanted to take a nap. While she slept, I decided to call a few of my auto dealers I've dealt with over the years to see if I could get a better quote than the one the dealership gave Florence. Luckily, I found a compressor for only two hundred fifty dollars. I had the company ship it to me overnight. After Florence had taken her nap, we drove around the city, went shopping at the Mall, and then headed back home to watch a couple movies. It was the best time I'd had in years. The following day when Florence was packing up to leave, I told her to not forget the package at the doorway. Florence said "What is it?" I said, "It's your AC compressor. I found one while you slept. The only thing your dad would have to do is, find someone to install it when you get home." Florence looked at me as if I'd just written her a million dollar check. I could tell she wasn't accustomed to anyone doing things for her. Florence looked at me with tears in her eyes and said "My dad would reimburse you." I said, "Consider the part a gift. Your dad doesn't owe me anything. Just make sure he pays someone to install the part." Florence wrapped her arms around me and kissed me ever so gently and said. "I will be leaving now. As much as I hate to go, I must. I will be in touch." Florence drove away, but in a sense, she seem to have left a part of herself to remind me the greatness God had in store for me.

Every thirty minutes, I would call Florence to see if she was okay. She would always say "I'll be fine from here on out." In her own way, I think she meant that literally. Days later, I thought I would call to check on her, but was unable to reach her. Weeks would go by and no sign of Florence anywhere. Weeks lead to months, months lead to years. I would call her phone, no response. I wrote letters to her, still no response. I thought she may have fallen off the face of the earth and none of her relatives knew my number to inform me of the tragedy. I started to think this woman was merely a dream, and meeting her was too good to be true. However, meeting her lead me to start writing Poetry again. I wanted to write about this beautiful dream I was presented. So I wrote and wrote.

"Five Years later"

Nathan

Florence showed up five years later and started our last conversation as if she'd simply taken a break to use the restroom. I asked her where did she go to. Her response was "I didn't go anywhere." I kept telling myself Florence was living a double life of some sort, but I didn't want to walk away from someone with such a beautiful soul and spirit based solely on my own suspicions. Whenever she would resurface, she would share hilarious stories about her Ex' Bobby. I never did understand how she felt so comfortable talking to me about him, but I would listen to her stories nevertheless. Florence told me a story once that still cracks me up to this day. She told me she and a co-worker (Rose) had been working together at the same job for years. She said Rose pulled her to the side one day and told her she and Bobby had been sleeping together for years, and because of their close relationship on the job, she felt she should know the truth. Florence said initially she didn't believe Rose. So Rose suggested that since they both got off work at the same time, they should ride together over to Bobby's house to prove her point. Florence said she thought it might be a good idea since Rose drove an SUV with dark tinted windows. She said she thought the tint, as awkward as it might seem, would help disguise the pain and disgust she was going through. Florence said during the drive over to Bobby's house, Rose told her those nights when Bobby lied and said he wasn't feeling well or gave her a lame excuse as to why he would be going to bed early, those were the nights he would sleep at her place. Florence told me the closer they got to Bobby's house, the deeper her heart began to sink. Florence said when Rose turned onto Bobby's driveway, Bobby and a group of guys were shooting dice. It was obvious Bobby had just won because he was excited with a fist full of five-dollar bills. As they drove up, Florence said Bobby stopped the game momentarily and started to approach the driver's side of the car. Florence said she'd

already felt like a fool by what she'd learned from Rose during the drive over, so she thought she would do something out of the ordinary that would help blow off the steam she had built up. Florence said she let her window down, stuck her head out and screamed as loud as she could at Bobby. "What in the hell are you trying to prove. She yelled." Bobby was shocked. He stood motionless, Florence said. Rose then opened her door and told Bobby that she'd told Florence everything that went on between them over the years.

Florence said, "Bobby responded by doing the unthinkable. He looked at his friends that were laughing at him profusely, scratched the top of his head, looked Rose straight in the eye and said, "I've never seen this bitch before in my life." Florence said she knew Rose had told her the truth, and it made her so sick to her stomach, all she could do was sit back in the passenger's seat and not burst with anger. Meanwhile, Florence said Rose walked up to Bobby and slapped him so hard, she thought his teeth had fallen out from the impact. Florence and I laughed so hard about this story. Unfortunately, Florence said she still dated him off and on despite how he was. She would always say to me, "I was stuck on stupid." I kept my opinions to myself, but deep inside, I couldn't agree with her more.

The disappearing acts of Florence had started to take a toll on me. I'd become weary of dealing with this type of relationship altogether. A part of me felt she would always be crazy in love with Bobby. So whenever she would resurface again, I wasn't as excited to see her as I once was. Nor was I as romantic with her as she'd grown accustomed to. She would ask, "What is wrong baby?" I was honest with her. I told her I was tired of not knowing where she disappears to, I'm tired of putting my other friends on the back-burner when she come around and more importantly, I would prefer to have someone that wants more of a committed relationship, and lastly, I'm tired of being tired." I'm not sure what I meant to Florence, but whatever feelings she had for me, she didn't want to lose it. For the very first time, she gave me an invite to her house in Beacon. I was shocked. Florence said "I would've given you an invitation sooner, but I wasn't sure you'd be up for the not-so-fun drive." I pondered over this idea for about two weeks. I decided I wouldn't give up on her just yet. I thought it was quite interesting that she gave me an invite when I was ready to 'throw in the towel'. Though I was partly over Florence's awkward ways, there was a part of me still intrigued. So I gave her a call and told her I would accept her invitation and would be visiting her the upcoming weekend. She thought

it would be perfect because she was off as well, she said. From Savannah, I took highway 321 to Pretzel, S.C. which was a boring drive to say the least. It was then I realized neither of my cell phones had service. I may have driven five minutes through the town, and before I knew it, I was out of the town limits. Miles further I ran into what look like a huge forest. This is the area Florence had warned me that the trees are humongous and the wildlife is incredibly huge. The deeper into the woods I drove, the more respect I gained for Florence. I even started to think she might actually like me after all. I couldn't imagine taking this drive at night to visit her if she ever asked... This drive was eerie for more than one reason. I was concerned about not having phone service, and the size of the deer I saw crossing the road way didn't make matters easier. I prayed hard and long that nothing goes wrong before I reach my destination.

"Our First Meeting at Her Place"

I must've driven another forty-five minutes before I finally reached a convenience store. I could hardly wait to ask the clerk what was up with the lack of phone service in these areas. The clerk said, "The areas you just drove through don't have cell towers, but your phone should have service now sir." The clerk was right. I paid for my fountain drink and hopped back in my van. As I started to back out from the parking lot, I realize the directions Florence gave me to her house were nowhere to be found. Luckily I did have phone service. I called Florence to let her know the directions to her place got misplaced. Florence asked where I was. I described the store to her. She said excitedly, "Stay right there, you're not that far away. I will send my son Junior to get you." Ten minutes later, her Volvo pulled into the parking lot. Her son got out of the car, introduced himself, and told me to follow him. This kid had such good manners. I also noticed that Junior drove slowly, which is a rarity nowadays for teenagers. I could tell he was raised by good parents or a great group of people. I jumped back in my van and followed Junior as he'd asked. It seemed there was a right or left turn every five hundred feet. I'm certain that, even if I hadn't lost the directions Florence had given me, I would've gotten lost eventually. We finally arrived at what looked like a small, white mansion. Junior parked his mom's car and ran over to tell me that I could park anywhere. There was plenty of room everywhere. I parked, got out of my van, and saw Florence running towards me with that familiar smile. This young lady's smile was so bright; it seemed as if I could see my future from her reflection. Florence formally introduced me to her son and proceeded to show me around. Junior then sat on the edge of the porch, as if he was an author gathering his thoughts. As Florence was showing me around, I couldn't help but notice a worn out basketball sitting on the side with a bent basketball goal tilted to the right. I thought Junior may have been dunking from only one side. I had a sudden urge to take a shot or two to see if I still could make a fifteen foot

jump-shot the way I once could. I grabbed the basketball, took aim, and fired an air-ball. Florence was tickled. She shook her head and said, "Let me show you how it's done." She must've hit ten consecutive shots. Then she spun the ball on her fingers like a Globetrotter and said, "This is a game you could never beat me at." On this particular day, she was right.

At Florence's House"

Nathan

Florence told me she wanted to treat me to dinner to a very unique restaurant if I was up to it. I said, "Dear, I am more than ready for a hearty meal. I was so hungry during the drive, I almost ate the two cows that had the conversation about you when you came to visit me." Florence fell to her knees in laughter. Once she gathered herself, I asked Florence, "What type of restaurant are you taking me to?" Florence laughed even harder. I wasn't certain what I'd said that had her so tickled. I couldn't tell if it was my Gullah accent that had her bent over, or, if she heard the growl in my stomach yearning for a hot meal. Whatever the case was, Florence kept it to herself. Three to four miles down the roadway, Florence decided to tell me that the restaurant, "*Michael's*" isn't the most attractive place around, but the food is amazing. A mile further we pulled up to what seemed like an open field. Cars were parked all along the roadway. I could smell the food from the outside. Of course I'd never eaten at a place in the middle of the woods before, but I was too hungry to critique anything at this point. We walked inside. The place was packed. The clerk was so kind and hospitable. We ordered Pulled barbecue Pork platters. It was by far the best Barbecue I've ever tasted. The food and service was an A-plus. Our bill was only twenty-five dollars. Florence paid our bill, so I thought the least I could do was place a twenty-five dollar tip in the clerk's hand. The clerk was so excited for the tip; she asked if she could give me a hug to show how appreciative she was. Weird I thought, but I agreed. Florence later told me that folks around these parts don't usually leave a tip like that. I told Florence I was just paying my blessings forward. As we drove back from our pleasing dining experience, Florence mentioned she would search for 'Suites' along our drive back. I said, "Dear, my tummy is so full right now, I couldn't handle dessert if you shoved it down my throat." Florence said, "No, I meant Suite as in

hotel. " I wondered for a split second why would we need a suite when she has a mansion, but decided to see how this whole thing plays out. Florence stopped at an elegant Suite two miles from her house. "This is the nicest suite in Beacon. I will pay for it if you didn't bring enough money." she said. "I brought my credit card and cash, I replied. Florence went inside to purchase a room and returned with the key. She handed the key over to me and said, "I will only be able to stay for an hour or so, then I'd have to get back home." I remember Florence telling me she was off the entire weekend, so I wasn't sure what to think at this point. I had more than a few questions that needed answers, but I didn't want to ruin my first visit by being so inquisitive. So I hid my emotions and refrained from the questions. It was hard to believe this was the same woman that clings to me like cotton when she visits me in Savannah. Maybe over the past five years she'd taken a religious approach and forgot to inform me, I assumed. I had a thousand thoughts running through my head. More than anything, I felt I could've stayed home and slept in my own bed instead of spending two hundred dollars to sleep alone. I didn't want to be petty and spoil my first visit, but I was not a happy camper by any means. In the back of my mind, I felt my first trip to Beacon might actually be my last.

"The Next Morning"

The next morning I was awakened by a phone call from Florence. She asked if I would join her for breakfast. Although I was still somewhat upset about spending the night alone, I thought a good breakfast might be easier to digest than the possibility of sleeping alone again in an unfamiliar area. I packed my belongings and drove over to Florence's house, where she had prepared an outstanding breakfast of everything I told her I enjoy eating at day-break. Florence had freshly-squeezed Orange Juice, Grits, Wheat Toast, breakfast sausages, and an Omelet so mouth-watering, it looked as if it was prepared by a professional Chef. The meal was not only appealing to my eyes, but equally fulfilling to my appetite. After I was done eating, I thanked Florence for everything, kissed her on the cheek (which was something I'd never done) and told her I was heading back to Savannah. "I thought you were off for the entire weekend," Florence said. I replied, "I thought you were also, but it doesn't seem like the case at all, So I think it might be an ideal time to go home, tune up my sports car and do some cleaning around my apartment," I said. Florence let out a sharp reply, "Fine then. You do just that." I wanted to tell her the real reason was that I didn't want to pay another two hundred dollars to sleep in a suite alone, but I thought it would be best if I stuck to the story I made up about the chores I wanted to take care of back home. I could tell Florence wasn't so thrilled that I was leaving after only one night, but a part of me didn't really care what she felt. I was still upset and confused as to why she invited me over in the first place if she had other reservations. As I got back in my van to head home, Florence stood in the drive-way until I pulled off. I wasn't so sure what her plans were for the weekend, but judging from her attitude, she may have had plans that included me. Nevertheless, I backed out of her drive-way and spun away, hoping she'd get the idea that I was still upset. Once I got onto the road, my intent was to slow down a bit so I could gather my thoughts on what I would do with the rest of my weekend. My head was spinning a thousand miles per hour it seemed. I had no idea where Florence and I would end up. Every other mile or so, my thoughts would become more cloudy than before. I got so caught up in my thoughts, that I didn't see the police car sitting in a ditch as I cruised by at eighty miles-per-hour. The officer got behind me, pulled me over, and asked for my license and registration. I handed my documents over to him. The officer looked them over and said, "Boy, where are you going so fast?" I said, "Sir, I just experienced something odd with my lady friend, lost my focus, and didn't realize I was traveling at such a high speed." The officer wrote me a ticket for one hundred seventy-seven dollars, handed it to me, and said, "Maybe you can pay this fine expeditiously as well." For a split second, I felt he was being sarcastic, or, perhaps Florence may have sent him after me because of the way I sped away from her thirty minutes earlier. Needless to say, I had a long drive back to Savannah. The beautiful farm that caught my attention on my drive to Beacon was merely a blur on my drive back. Florence called a few times to check on me during my drive. I told her I would be fine and would call her once I got home to let her know I was safe. I kept our conversations short. I'm sure Florence thought I was being petty, and to some degree, maybe I was, but it was my way of showing her I didn't appreciate getting an invitation to sleep in a suite all alone. Once I got home, I called Florence to let her know I was safe and told her I would get back with her... We spoke briefly the next two days, but each following day thereafter our conversations became less and less. I truly believe it was my stubbornness and insecurities, combined with Florence's reluctance to return phone calls that led us to not have another conversation again for five years.

Chapter Three

Nathan

Time passed so quickly, I'd almost forgotten why I was so upset at Florence the past five years. As attractive as she was, there was an oddity about her I never could understand. She would disappear for long periods at a time and would never reveal where she disappears to. Because of that, as much as I wanted to, I never could give all of myself to her. A part of me felt Florence either worked for the CIA or she may have lied to me about being single. Sometimes while we were apart, I would reflect back over our fun times and some of the stories she did reveal to me. I thought maybe somewhere in the midst of one of her stories she may have mistakenly mentioned the reason she constantly disappears, but I realized she has always chosen her words wisely. I got tired of trying to figure Florence out. I prayed on the situation and decided to let nature take its course. Instead of reading into my thoughts, I would re-read some of the poems I'd written over the years just to reminisce.

"My Heart"

'I have followed my heart on many occasions and lost. I've followed my mind several times and lost as well. But whenever I went with my instincts, I won every time. Yet, I would go with my

heart again, not because I'm stubborn, simply because I am certain, I would get to learn something valuable, time and time again.'

"A Letter for Florence"

'Today I found myself reflecting on the very first time you and I met. It gave me a reason to smile. I smiled because I remember being mesmerized by your beauty and equally impressed with the accent and eloquence in which you spoke. You were like a glow of sunshine on a rainy day. You lit my inner self and gave me a sense acknowledgment that angels do walk on earth. I didn't always believe in earth angels, but I've always known God has a way of allowing us to meet people that would give us a sense of intrigue, hope, and admiration. I find all of these things in you. Contrary to popular belief, it is said that men don't usually pay attention to certain things. Well, maybe I am unique because, as you slowly walked towards me, I noticed your perfectly-lined lip gloss, the rhythm in each step you took, I visibly measured your body measurements to a tee. And I even tried to count every strand of hair on your eyebrow. However, my purpose wasn't to prove everyone wrong, but more so to reassure myself that, if I were to encounter another angel as beautiful as you, I wouldn't be swept away in the same manner as our first encounter. I'd like to seal this letter with a sense of hope. I hope the rest of the world finds you as attractive as I have. And if by chance this doesn't happen, it would give me hope that you may have been created just for me.'

"Lessons of a Leaf"

'Some friends are like leaves on a tree. They will get blown away from the slightest wind, some will fall on their own because they didn't want to witness your growth, and others will fall because they weren't suppose to be part of the process. Look to your left. If the ones you've done right by are no longer there, this is a lesson, not a loss. They were there to teach you the difference. Now look to your right. If you find people still standing there after you've been through your toughest storms, these are ones you should cherish throughout your growth and beyond.'

"Dreams"

'I have dreamed many dreams. Some I pursued to the very end, others I may have lost for having such a lackadaisical approach. But I always know my eagerness to pursue those dreams unfulfilled would re-emerge one day. I just pray they would still be available to me when I do. And if by chance they're not, I will accept the fact that, either those things weren't meant for me at all, or, God wanted to present them to me when he was certain I'd be able to appreciate and understand that their values were equally as important as their beauty.'

"A Poem Pending"

'Sometimes, while the rest of the world is still asleep, at least a thousand beautiful thoughts come to mind that I'd like to express on paper just for you. But in the midst of writing, it seem as if the world wakes up and distracts me, leaving me with beautiful, unexplained ideas, and an unfulfilled desire. So until there's nothing but pure silence and serenity, I will retain those thoughts, with hopes that one day, they will become soothing music to your ears.'

As much as I hated to admit it, Florence had become my ray of light. On rainy days, she seemed to be my umbrella. Those years while she and I were apart, there was a part of me that felt her presence as if she was standing right beside me. There were times I would listen to love songs by Luther Vandrous and Smokey Robinson and would reflect on the very first time we danced. She held me long after each song was finished, kissed me ever so gently and would whisper "I don't ever want to let you go." I didn't know how serious Florence was at the time, so I didn't put a lot of emphasis on her sensuous comments. I would learn later on that she meant every word. Smokey Robinson had a song out called "*Easy To Love.*" Every lyric in the song reminded me of Florence. She was easy to love and hard to forget. I would play this song so much while I was at work; my co-workers said they'd turn their radios off if that song started playing while they were driving home. I was so into her that I'd made up my mind that when she does come back around, I would even accept her disappearing act as long as she continued to pamper me the way she's always done. I believe a part of me liked the fact that whenever Florence would return, she would treat to upscale restaurants, Museums across the South, and all-expense paid shopping sprees throughout South Carolina and Georgia coast. And whenever I'd have weekends off, she would treat me to college football games all over the country. Her favorite football team was Wake forest. I never would forget the time Florence treated me to Orlando Florida as a vacation gift. We had a blast! She would always rent a villa whenever she took me out of town. She was classy like that. However, sometimes during these trips, we wouldn't say more than two words to each other during the entire trip, but we would have the best time ever once we reached our destination. I learned over time that Florence's actions would say more than she cared to speak on.

"New Beginnings"

So accustomed to prior years, I'd gotten used to the five-year gaps in our relationship. So I was patiently waiting when, much to my surprise, Florence called. It had been only three years since I last heard from her, so this was a pleasant surprise indeed. Florence said, "Hello dear, are you ready to marry me?" Totally shocked, I said "Marry you? I hardly ever see you. I would first need to find someone that knows what love is, and doesn't just love in five-year increments." Florence said "Nathan, I love you and you know it. So if you love me, prove it. And while you're thinking about it, I've already purchased the center where we'd be getting married. So, are you ready?" I didn't react right away. I had so many questions I needed Florence to answer. I needed to know first and foremost if she was serious. Secondly, I wasn't sure if I wanted to marry someone that disappears for five years at a time. I told Florence I would need a week or two to think things over and I will get back to her. I thought this idea of marriage over for two weeks. I knew I was getting older and so was she. I thought about Florence's incomparable qualities, her smile, how well she paid attention to my likes and dislikes, and the way she pampered me when comes in town. I weighed the good and bad. I happened to realize that her only bad habit was the disappearing acts. I figured her good far out-weighed the bad. I also realized that I'd dated women with a lot more problems, so marrying Florence can't be the end of the world. I called her to let her know that I'd made my decision and we could set a date for the occasion. We set our wedding date for September 18th two-thousand eight. Florence was elated. She called every single family member she could think of to share our big news. I too called a few of my family members. I got mixed opinions of course. My family thought I should be a bit precautious because this woman could very well be a 'Gold-Digger.' Well, my thoughts were, my family doesn't know my wife-to-be as well as I do. And besides, I don't posses any Gold. My intuition told me I'd be doing the right thing if I marry Florence. Though I'd never

met anyone that would purchase a place to get married without discussing it with their other half, I proceeded on. I thought I would ask Florence to move in with me at my new place on Hilton Head Island to see if marriage would be the ideal thing for us. Florence agreed to move in with me. Even though Hilton Head was beautiful, clean, and crime-free for the most part, I wasn't sure how the transition would be for Florence, coming from the red clays of Beacon to the sandy beaches of the island. Within three days, Florence had moved her belongings in, and we started our life together on lovely Hilton Head Island South Carolina. I went out to 'Exquisite Diamonds' in savannah to purchase a ring for my new bride. The clerk in the store was an older Black woman, whom I'd never met before in my life. The clerk walked over and introduced herself as 'Ms. Ann.' Even though she was an old woman, I detected a sense of wisdom from the very moment she said hello. While I was gazing at the many beautiful diamonds in the jewelry case, Ms. Ann walked over and said, "I know why you're here. You are here to purchase a gift for the young lady you've been dealing with for so many years. The young lady is deserving of the gift you're about to purchase, and she will treasure it like no other, but she can't reciprocate at the time, her hands are tied. She do love you and one day she will sit down with you and tell you the very reason you couldn't have all of her the way she'd want. She will answer all of the questions you've never had answers for." I started to feel somewhat eerie, so I decided to walk away for a brief moment to process this unwanted information.

Ms. Ann walked over, looked me in the eyes and said, "Sir, please don't interrupt the young lady when she finally opens up to you. She will tell you things she's always wanted to say but couldn't find the words or courage to say them. I would advise you to just sit and listen. This will be the moment she's always wanted. Now, how else may I help you sir?" I heard every word Ms. Ann had said, but none of it made any sense to me. I felt she may have mistaken me for someone else. At least I was hoping she had.

I was in total shock, to say the least. I finally gathered my composure and asked Ms. Ann, "Which of these rings in this jewelry case would sweep my new bride off of her feet?" Ms. Ann replied, "Sir, you've already swept the young lady off her feet. In her eyes, you are unique in every way. She has never met anyone like you. But because of her situation, she cannot reciprocate the way she'd like to. She loves you dearly, but she has a 'Bug in her bed-sheet." I wasn't too keen on cliché's, nor was I interested in anything else Ms. Ann had to say. I figured if I listened to her any longer, I might end up not purchasing a ring at all. So I looked over the ring I would purchase, a half-carat diamond with two emeralds, one on each side. The ring was a size'9, (Florence's finger size exactly). I purchased the ring, thanked Ms. Ann for the alarming words and made my way back to Hilton Head. Later that night I gave Florence the ring I'd purchased. Florence was so excited, she couldn't stop crying. Once she finally got herself together, she called her family members to share the news of her new gem. She must've called two hundred family members that night. I fell asleep and woke up a few hours later to find her asleep in the love-seat, holding the ring to her chest with both hands. I woke Florence to let her know she'd fallen asleep in her nurse's uniform and she needed to get adequate rest. Besides, she had just recently started her new job at the local hospital and it wouldn't be a good look going to work exhausted her first week. Florence agreed. She showered, got in bed, with the ring in tow, as if someone might steal it. I thought it was odd but I didn't want to ruin her night.

For several months, everything had become a matter of adjustments. We both were accustomed to our own way of thinking, likes and dislikes. It took us awhile but we finally learned to compromise. Whenever our timing would coincide, I would treat Florence to upscale restaurants, just as she'd done for me in years past. We would take walks on different beaches after dinner, or sometimes go to watch a movie or two at Mid-Island. As happy as I was with Florence, I could tell she didn't share the same contentment. Months later Florence would surprise me by attending engagements or so-called church events in Beacon without inviting me. She would return three to four hours later, eyes swollen from fatigue. I didn't want to speculate or be judgmental, but I knew something was definitely not right.

For the next few months, I would check my caller ID nightly. I noticed Bobby had been calling constantly for the past two weeks. My first thought was, maybe it's their way of finding closure, so I didn't bother asking her why Bobby had my telephone number. I noticed also that each call between them was over two hours. Well, I couldn't restrain myself any longer. I sat Florence down after her shift ended the following day and said, "I am not feeling the same way I felt months earlier. Also, my intuition is telling me there's a story brewing neither of us would be happy with the ending. And more importantly, I want no part of a wedding whatsoever." Florence looked at me as if she'd seen a ghost, or perhaps I'd found out what she'd been doing behind closed doors. I could tell Florence was shaken by my comment. Her eyes got full of tears. After a long pause, she said, "Well, if you feel that way about it, I will move back home to Beacon with hopes that you'd change your mind one day." I was so upset; the only thing that came to mind was a sharp reply. I said, "I would almost bet my life I won't ever change my mind Florence." I didn't even ask for the ring back. I just wanted Florence gone. She packed her belongings, hopped in her car and drove away. I didn't even say goodbye. Even though I never witnessed with my own eyes that Florence was still seeing Bobby, my intuition was speaking loud and clear.

Chapter Four

Nathan

Florence would call every now and then, but I would keep our conversations at a minimum. Even though time had slipped on by, I was still bitter towards Florence. I felt I'd given her everything I could, and she was ungrateful. So whenever she would ask if I would come to visit her, I would come up with an excuse. Then I got tired of lying to her and making up excuses. So one day while I was driving my sports car through the small town of Bluffton, Florence called my cell. I looked at my phone, saw it was her, and I threw my cell right out the window. I know the phone was our only line of communication. So now I had a sigh of relief. The following month I joined a pool league in the Hilton Head/ Bluffton area. I also started to write Poetry again. I even laced up my tennis shoes again and started playing basketball just to keep my mind occupied. I played a lot of basketball with friends such as T. Mikell, J. Miller, 'Smiley' Hudson, Lawrence O, and J. Stewart, just to name a few. Before I knew it, I was back in shape in two months, won an 'Eight-Ball tournament, and wrote and published two books. With no lines of communication from Florence, and my mind focused, I had success at everything I set out to do. I used the experience from my relationship with Florence for inspiration. Some of my Poetry was directed towards Florence, others were simply random thoughts or insights like;

"Value"

'I try not to put so much value on people or things I know will depreciate over time. Instead, I treasure people that had an impact on my life in some capacity. Whether or not we say 'Goodbye' or 'Goodnight' today doesn't matter. Simply because those moments spent have a lasting effect that speaks for itself, and carries a lifespan that won't ever expire.'

"In My Dreams"

'I have held you in my arms at least ten thousand times. You and I have traveled around the world and have played under waterfalls in distant regions. I've fed you grapes and shared several glasses of champagne with you on numerous occasions. I have prepared gourmet meals for you every afternoon since we began talking. Every night before bedtime, I've given you massages so therapeutic, it left you wishing the night would never end. And just so your wish would come true, I'd always end up being the reason as to why, in moments like these, sleep is frequently thrown out of the window.'

Exactly five years later, I logged onto my facebook account. I realized Florence had sent me a friend- request. I didn't know what to think at this point. I pondered over accepting her request for an entire week. I finally decided to accept her request to see what she had to say. Florence told me she'd been sick. She said she had a heart condition, but she needed to speak with me face to face to disclose some other matters of importance. I could swear she wanted to kill me for avoiding her all this time. I ran the idea of meeting with Florence by one of my co-workers, Rodney, who was fully aware of our relationship. Rodney thought Florence might be sincere about being sick and might just wanted closure. My mean side was a bit apprehensive about meeting with Florence, but my compassionate side thought the least I could do was meet with her, particularly if she was telling the truth about being sick. I agreed to have Florence meet with me at my villa. I wasn't sure what to expect. I even thought about purchasing a bullet-proof vest to be on the safe side. But instead, I prayed to God for protection. I went downstairs and waited for Florence in the parking lot. She must've hopped in her car immediately because exactly two and a half hours later, Florence was pulling up in my parking lot. Florence wore a sundress, which made the scars from her surgery conspicuous. She parked her car, got out and embraced me with the warmest hug ever. She was as beautiful as the first night I met her in Savannah. Any animosity I had towards Florence dissipated immediately. I took her to dinner. We ordered, and while our dinner was being prepared, Florence started the conversation with an apology for her ungratefulness when we were together. Florence said, "I wanted to apologize sooner but I'm sure you didn't care to hear anything I had to say and I was hoping time would be in our favor and we could sit down and talk things over." I didn't know how genuine she was, so I just said, "Go on." I gave Florence my full attention, as I've always done. Florence told me that when she and I went our separate ways, she started dating Bobby on a regular basis. She said the relationship lasted all of one month. I briefly interrupted, "What happened?" Florence said, "I knew it

was waste of energy from the beginning, but I needed something or someone to make me feel worthy after the way you sent me packing." Florence continued, "However, I learned the hard way that those bad choices I'd made would come back to haunt me in a way I couldn't have imagined. Florence said, "Two years later, I met a classmate from back in my high school days. We got engaged and I moved him in my house." Congratulations", I mumbled. Florence said, "Oh that relationship didn't work either. He decided to quit his job thinking he didn't have to work again, so I packed his belongings, took them over to his mother's house, and haven't seen him since." I was like "What in the world." Florence laughed, but suddenly that laughter changed to tears. Florence said, "Nathan, you were the perfect guy. I always knew this, but I just couldn't reciprocate the way I wanted to.

"Our Final Walk"

Nathan

Our meal finally arrived. I didn't have much of an appetite, but I ordered a Pasta dish just so Florence wouldn't be eating alone. I watched as Florence ate her heart away. I remember her telling me the first time she visited me in Savannah that the way to her heart was through a hearty meal. Her comment seemed to hold true after all those years.

When Florence was done with her meal, I asked her "What was so important that we had to meet face to face?" Florence pushed her plate to the side and uttered these words, "Nathan, please don't change who you are. You are the perfect man. I knew this all along. My parents also felt this way. I wanted to give you my all but wasn't able to. The only reason you and I didn't make it was because I was still seeing Bobby while I was trying to make it with you." I looked at Florence in disbelief, not because I didn't believe her, but merely because it had been five years. In the back of my mind, that could've been a well-kept secret. There was no way I could've found out even if I wanted to. I asked Florence "Why after five years you want to reveal this? Florence said, "I wanted to confess this all along, but I know you didn't care to hear anything I had to say and I prayed to God to grant me the opportunity and nerve to open up to you." For one of the few times in my life, I was left speechless. I gathered my breath and asked Florence did she even love me back then. Florence quickly responded, "Nathan, I love you still. I'm sure you couldn't see it through all of the confusion I put you through back then, but I'd even confessed my love for you to my family and Bobby years ago." It was getting late. I paid our tab and asked Florence if there was anything else she'd like to share while she had my full attention. Florence said, "As a matter of fact, there is. I would like you to take me near the beach. I need to feel the water." Well, my villa was only a few blocks away from the beach, so taking her for a splash was only two minutes away.

Once we got to the beach, I ordered two 'Mango Daiquiris'. After we finished our drinks, I walked with Florence near the shoreline. I said to Florence, "Don't get too close to the water, because if a shark should attack, I won't be able to save you." Florence burst out in laughter. She then said to me rather passionately, "I know without a shadow of a doubt, you'd save me." Florence walked along the shore as I stood a few feet away. She knelt down, put both hands in the water, stood up and let the water run down her arms. Florence then looked at me, with tears in her eyes and said "I am ready to go home now." For some strange reason, my eyes also became full. I took Florence by the hand, walked her to the car and headed back to my place. When we pulled into my parking space, Florence said, "Nathan, there's one other favor I'd like to ask of you before I drive away." I said, "Sure, what is it?" Florence said, "Nathan, I am having another surgery for my heart next week. I'm not sure I will survive this surgery, but if you could be there during the procedure, I would be at peace whether I live or die." Totally caught off guard, I said to Florence, "Are you sure you want me at your side?" Florence said, "If I only had one day left on earth, I'd want you there beside me."

"Our Last Face to face Chat"

Nathan

Florence's words had me shook. I held my head down searching for the right words to say. It seemed I had a thousand questions to ask but the seriousness in Florence's eyes told me this wasn't the time to be inquisitive. Before I gave her a response, I asked myself two questions. One, how should I respond to such a request from someone I hadn't seen in five years? And secondly, would I be able to watch someone I adored for so many years suffer in pain and not be able to help? I held my head up to finally respond to Florence's request. I said, "Dear, I'd like to be there with you, but would prefer to send prayers by text message throughout your surgery and beyond." Florence looked at me as if she knew what my answer would be. Surprisingly, she just smiled and said "Dear, that would be perfect then." Florence got in her car to drive back to Beacon. I stood motionless as she revved the engine in her Chrysler Sebring. Florence downed her window and motioned me come a bit closer. She held my hand and uttered these words, "Nathan, I would like to apologize for everything I've done wrong during our time. I never meant to hurt you. I wish there was a way I could take back those foolish mistakes I've made, but you and I both know that can't happen. You are the most phenomenal man I've ever met. I'm so sorry I wasn't able to reciprocate the way I wanted to. As I look back, I realize I was caught up in what seemed like a perfect triangle at the time. My relationship with Bobby had long been over when I met you. He and I had become platonic friends. I compounded those mistakes by talking to him about you. I would tell him often how unique you are. He wasn't thrilled to hear about you, but he would listen nevertheless. Bobby and I lived only two miles away from one another. I foolishly allowed convenience to get in the way of something unique, special, and meaningful. I feel it was by far the biggest mistake I've ever made in my life. I have regrets every single day. I take full responsibility for why things didn't work out between me and you. All I can do now is ask that you please forgive me. Nathan, I'm not sure what God has planned for me, but I pray he has a way for you and I to cross paths again. Meanwhile, please keep me in your prayers. I will look for your prayers on my phone. I will say bye for now." I thanked Florence for her openness and honesty and told her all was forgiven.

Like old times, I called every thirty minutes to check on her during her drive back to Beacon. Florence and I had made amends. It was like a burden lifted off of me. I remember the look in Florence's eyes during her confessions. Before that day, she was never one to speak a whole lot, so I'd learned over time how to read her eyes. On this day, her eyes told me she was at peace. In all the years I'd known her, I'd never seen her so content and worry-free.

"Our Last Face to Face Chat"

Nathan

The following week finally arrived. Everything around me seemed to be moving in slow motion. I was concerned about Florence and the severity of her sickness. I thought it would be a good idea to Google Florence's dad, Bill's telephone number so he could keep me informed about his daughter's health, but I remembered my last conversation with him wasn't a friendly chat at the beach. So I did what I've always done when I had no one else to turn to. I got down on my knees and prayed to God. I prayed for Florence's surgery to go well, and while in prayer, I thanked God for allowing me the opportunity so that my friend and I could make amends. After I was done praying, I wrote down prayers so I could text them to Florence's phone. I started sending those messages every day after Florence's surgery. About a week later I got a text from Florence's phone. The message read, "Thank you so much for your prayers for our daughter." I thought I'd accidentally texted someone else's phone. I went over the message I'd sent to check to see if I'd made an error, but the number was the exact one Florence had given me to use. The following day I sent another prayer to the exact number with hopes I'd get a response that would make sense. About an hour later, a text message came through from Florence's phone again. It read, "*Nathan, this is Bill, Florence's dad. We've been reading your text messages to Florence because she is unable to do so herself after the surgery. She's asleep at the moment, but had asked the family to make sure we let you know she's okay. Please continue to send your prayers. Thank you, Bill.*" I felt a sense of relief for more reasons than one. Both of my concerns were answered. I now knew Florence's surgery went well, and I now know I didn't accidentally send a prayer-text to the wrong person's phone. I continued to send prayers every day on Florence' phone. The following two weeks, I didn't get any reply messages from Florence's dad. However, I wasn't overly concerned because

her surgery had gone well. A month later, I finally got a text from Florence's phone. This time it was from Florence's mother, Janie. Her message read, "*Nathan, please continue with your prayers. Florence needs them. She isn't feeling so well these days, she's been experiencing a lot of pain, but somehow your prayers seem to make her smile anyhow. So please continue to send them. Thanks, Janie.*"

"Months Later"

It was October two thousand sixteen, Hurricane Mathews was approaching the Carolina coast and everyone had to evacuate. I was scrambling around to get things organized when all of a sudden I dropped my cell phone, which shattered to pieces, leaving me unable to communicate with anyone throughout the entire evacuation process. I could no longer send prayers to Florence's phone nor did I have a way to let her or her family know the reason. Hurricane Mathews slammed the entire coast. I was stuck without a telephone for ten straight days. I could hardly wait for a phone company and the roadways to reopen so I could purchase another phone.

Ten days later, the stores, roadways, and businesses finally reopened. I bought another cell phone and kept the exact number so my messages would transfer onto the new number. Much to my dismay, there was a long message from Florence's dad that left me cold and numb. The message read, *"Nathan, this is Bill again. First and foremost, I'd like to commend you for your constant prayers for our daughter Florence. She fought a good fight but she Finally got tired of fighting. Weeks earlier, the entire family was at her house trying to get her reacclimated to her own house, where she'd lived for most of her life. After so many surgeries, a toll was being taken on her brains as well. She couldn't even recognize her own brother, who'd traveled from Boston or her two older sisters from Gathens Ga. which wasn't so surprising. However, what did surprise all of us is, she called everyone to her bedroom as she finally gathered enough strength to raise her head from the pillow. Everyone rushed to her bedside, where she asked all of us to do her a big favor.* Florence said, "Please, I need all of you to do whatever it takes, by any means necessary to contact Nathan so he'd know what is going on with me." *Her comment left my entire family in shock. We didn't understand how she couldn't remember her own sisters or brother whom she grew up with, but didn't forget you. For years Florence would tell the family that the love she has for*

you couldn't be explained in words. We would shake our heads and laugh. Well, I just want you to know, as a church- going man myself, not everything has to be explained. Florence's home going will be at 10.00am Monday morning. My family and I know she would be at peace knowing you are here in attendance during her service. We, the family, would like to commend you for being a true gentleman throughout. This phone would be deactivated in twenty-four hours. It would be a pleasure to speak with you within that time frame." **As soon as I got the message, I called the number Bill had left on my phone but, unfortunately, the phone just rang. I mailed a sympathy card with my condolences to Junior to let him know his loss was mine as well.**

I could only pray that my letter would help soothe the pain of loss that Florence's family had to endure. As I reflect back on everything, I now fully understand why they shook their heads when Florence spoke of her feelings. For more than seventeen years, I also had to shake my head a few times. It wasn't until Florence and I made amends, I was able to grasp what her true feelings were. Florence taught me a lot about love. She wasn't perfect, but in her own way, she tried to show me that our perfect moments would outlive our worst times. She taught me our heart doesn't always choose what is best for us, but every choice it makes should teach us something valuable. And most importantly, Florence showed me that, though none of us are perfect, for a little while, we all might be the perfect fit for someone else.

"Queen of Hearts"

'Nowadays I find myself looking towards the sky, with hopes that her lovely face would suddenly appear. But it isn't until I start to recite poems she once loved that, a hint of her perfume fills the area, allowing me to believe, she either still find it amusing that I stumble over my words, or, she came to remind me that, no matter how far away we are, my words resonates and still have a unique way of bringing her into my space.'

"People"

'People will try to judge you no matter what you do. So try to be so passionate about whatever it is you're doing, that even if they're not a fan, they would find themselves admiring your passion through your body of work'

"God is With Us All"

'One day you will look back at the many bumps in the road you withstood. You will smile because you would realize you were never alone at any point during your journey.'

"Roses Are We"

'In a sense, we are all a bunch of roses. We are fragile to the touch, we come in an assortment of different colors, and certainly some of us may have more thorns than others, but we are all one. We all flourish from the love and nourishment that keeps us alive. Yet, in the end, none of us will be judged by our petals or beauty, but merely those thorns we accumulated during our growth.

"Nathan's Angels"

"I Call Her a Rose"

'I remember when she was merely a bud
Fragile and so very young
Her stem grew, petals blossomed
She became the most beautiful flower under the sun,
Her eyes sparkled as if they were diamonds
Her smile was equally as bright
I often find myself admiring her photos during the day
Amazed at how I became her vase at night,
She might whisper softly to her friends
Saying she doesn't know to whom this poem refers
She might tell them it sounds much like an old song
Knowing all along it was exclusively written for her,
She might look her male friend in the eye
Tell him it's just an ordinary prose
He might sense there may be more to this story
But it's a tale neither she nor I are willing to disclose.

"Poets"

'We are considered ordinary people with an extraordinary and unique ability to combine our vivid imaginations and gift with passion, which ultimately defines our purpose.

Charitable Donations

A portion of the proceeds for this book will be donated for Cancer research.

"I Wouldn't Change Anything"

'If I could do it all over again, I wouldn't change the way I loved for one second. However, I would be a bit more apprehensive about trying to give love to those unwilling to give back.

"My Message To You"

Last October, soon after Hurricane Mathews, I decided to drive around a few towns to witness the mass destruction everyone had been talking about days earlier. I drove down Bluffton Parkway, then onto Hilton Head Island. Along the way, I stopped at the entrance to Port Royal, where massive trees had been uprooted. Folks had stopped and parked all along '278' to take pictures of the destruction. I chose to look instead at the smaller trees. Most of them I could bend with my bare hands. However, those smaller trees seemed untouched, not even a leaf was missing. At that moment, I realized something profound. Nothing happens before it's time. It doesn't matter how big of a tree one might be, or what they may have in their trunk, nothing happens before it's time. With that

being said, if you have a dream, vision, or certain aspiration you'd like to pursue, don't let anyone discourage you from doing so. Things may seem a bit dysfunctional in the beginning, you might experience days of doubt, but things wouldn't be as gratifying if they were easy. The person sitting next to you that said, "It can't happen", prove him wrong, the EX that prayed for you to fail, show him or her you won't be denied. Don't be afraid to make sacrifices if you must. Remember, what you're trying to attain shouldn't be easy, if it were, anyone could do it. Let your dreams be your motivation. People can purchase the same blouse or pants as you, they may even try to duplicate your style, but they can't ever say they had the exact dream. I pray this message finds someone searching for a sense of direction. Sometimes God has a way of sending messages through unlikely sources.

CPSIA information can be obtained
at www.ICGtesting.com
Printed in the USA
BVHW031343061119
563063BV00001B/58/P